Plant Parts

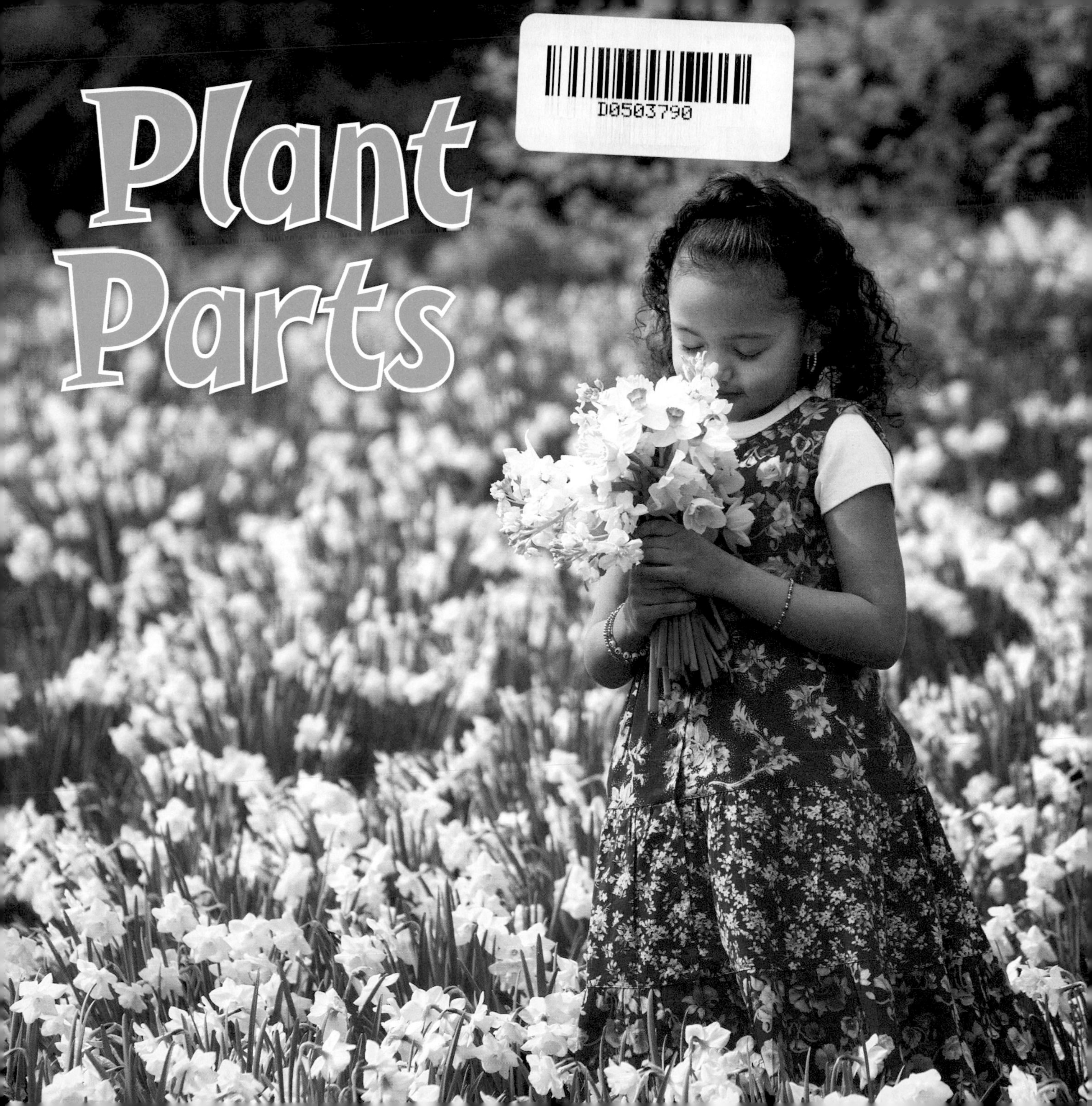

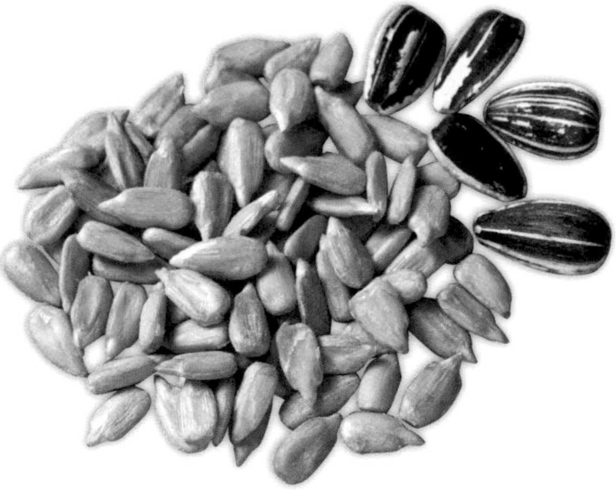

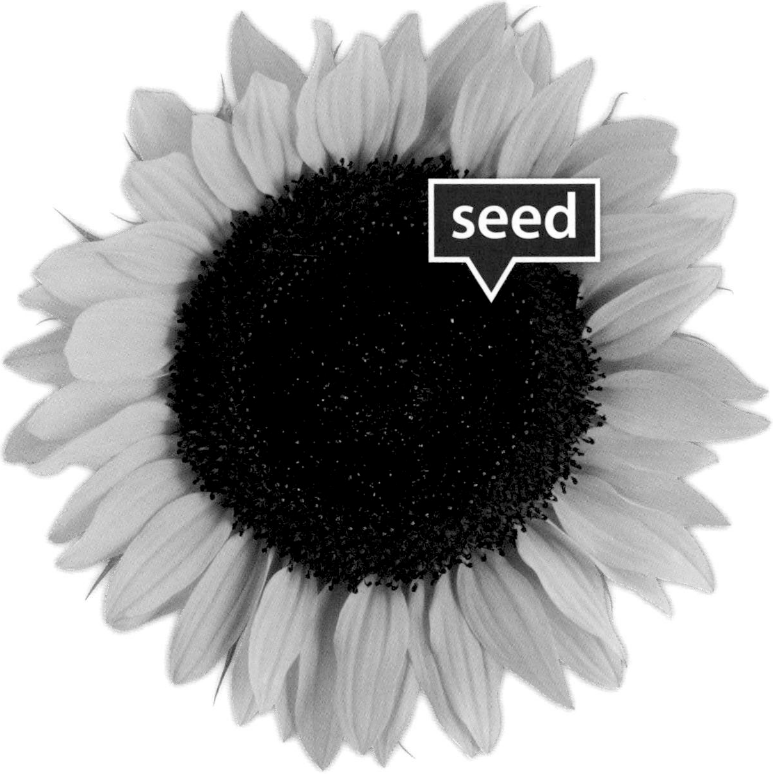

seeds

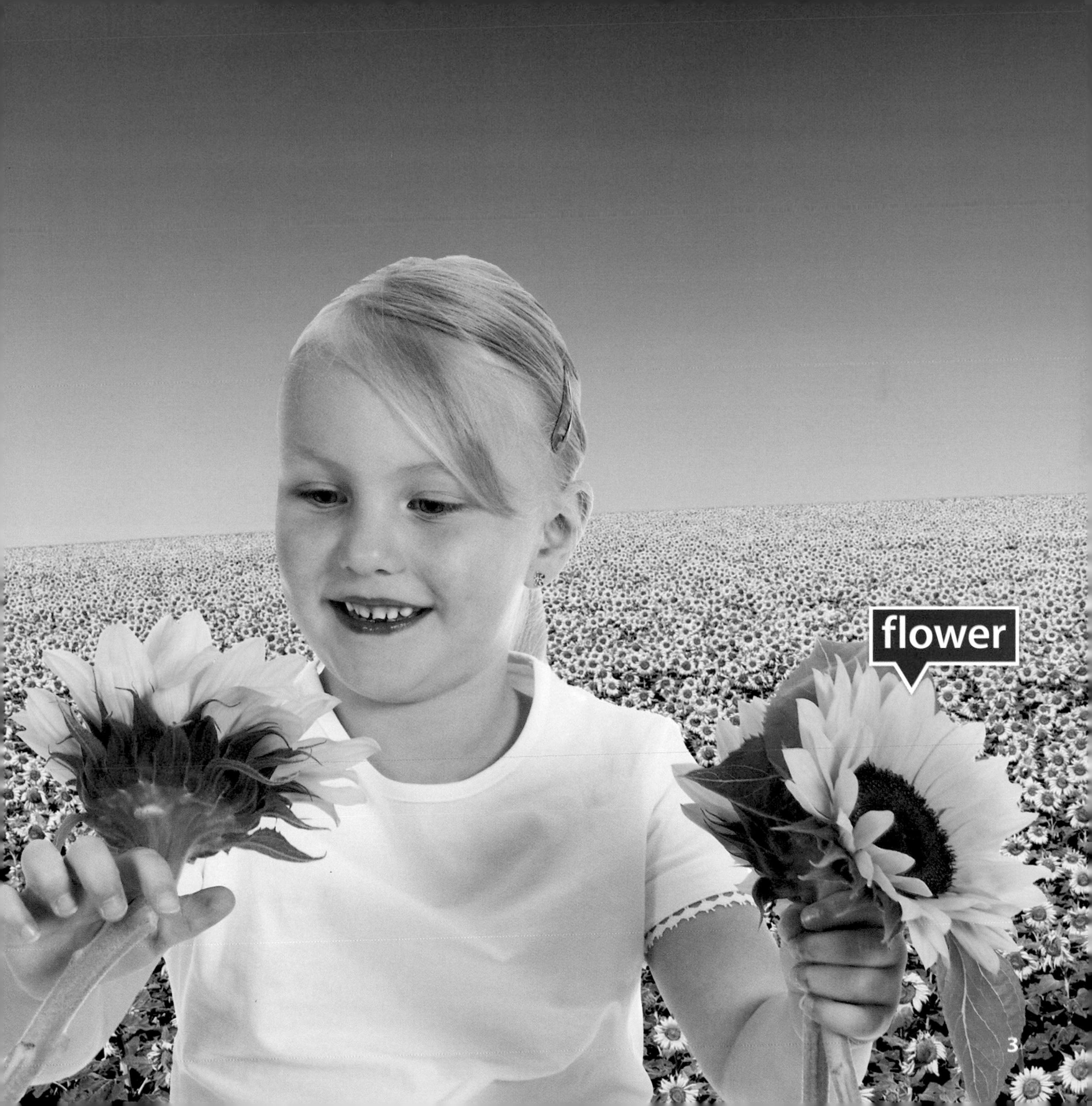
flower

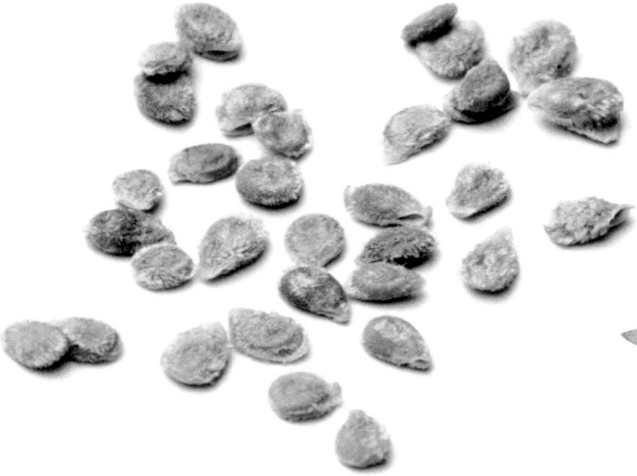

seeds

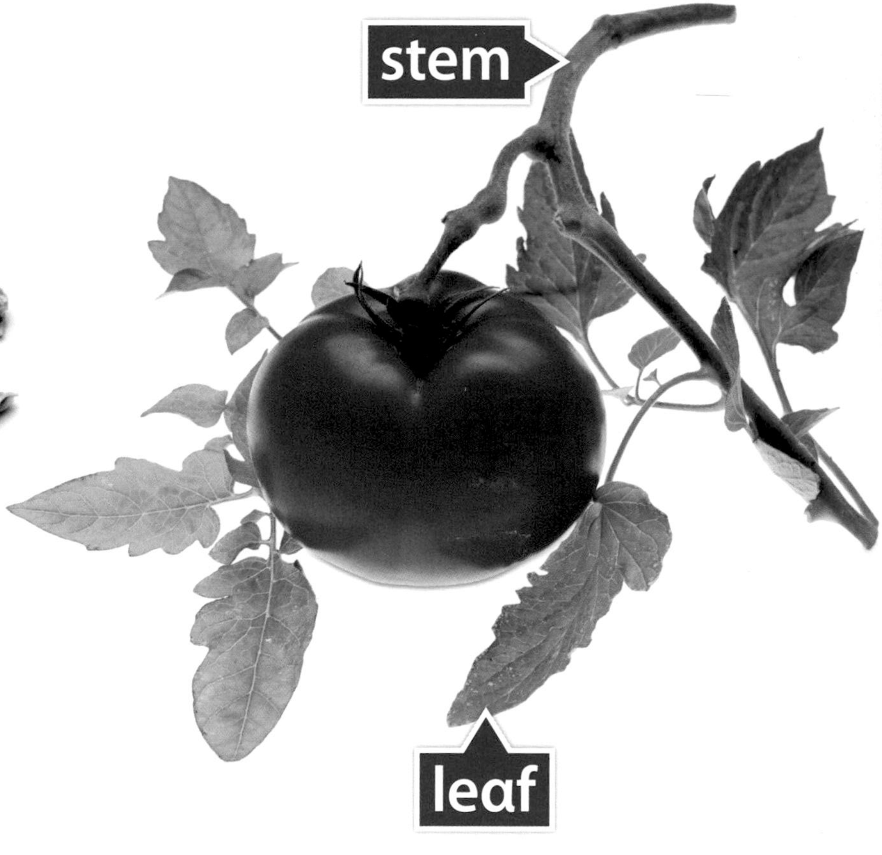

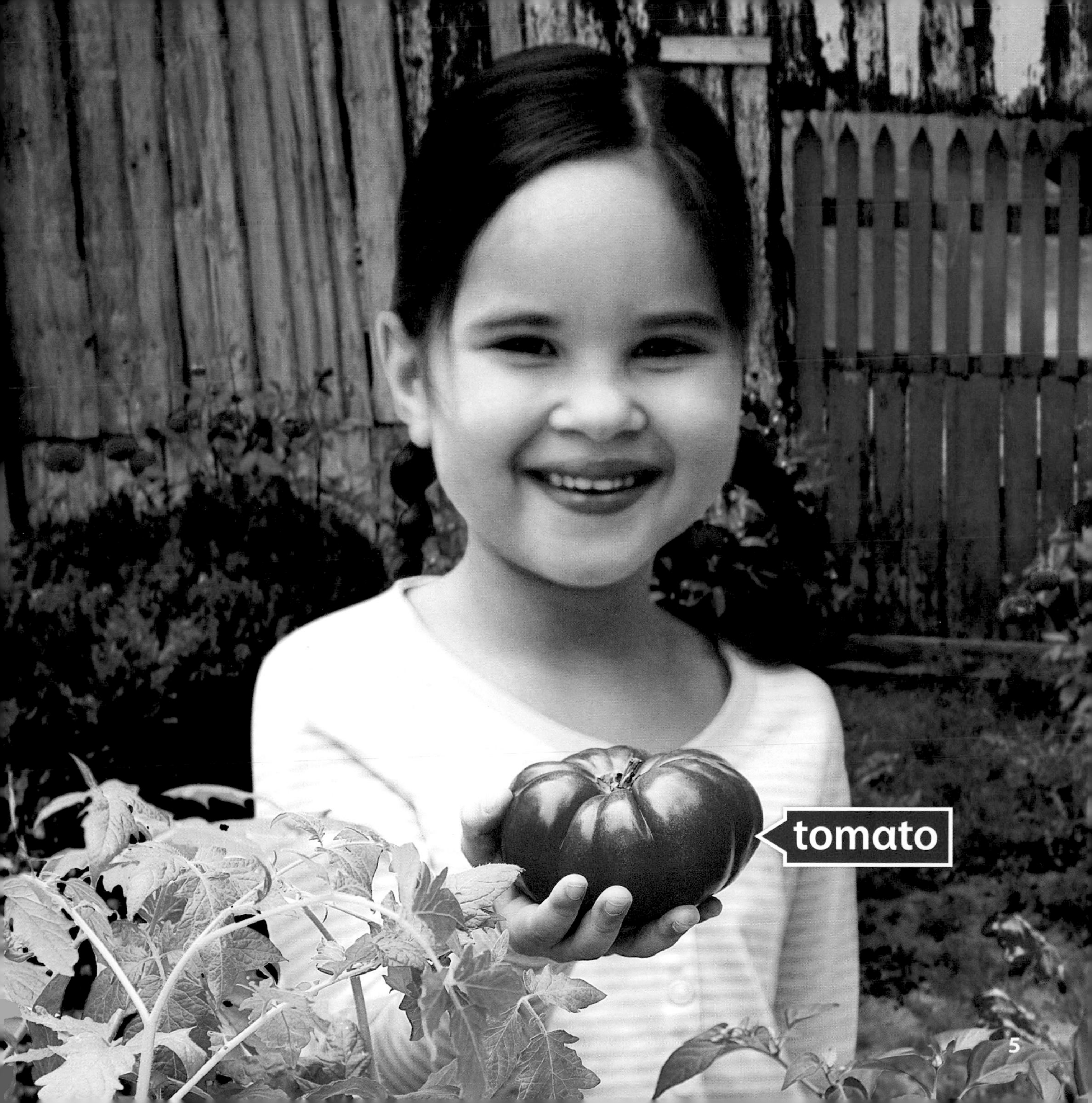
tomato

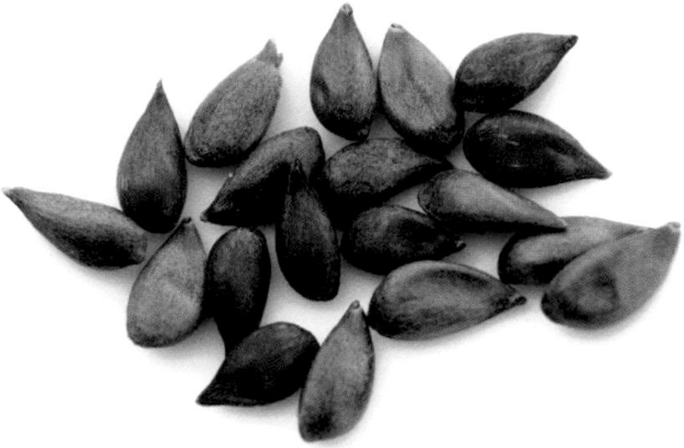

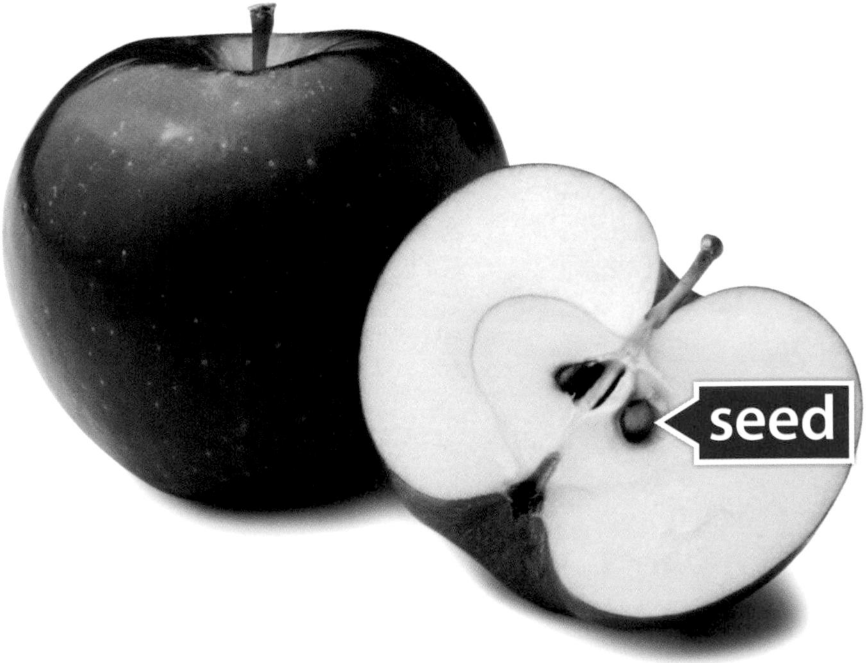

seeds

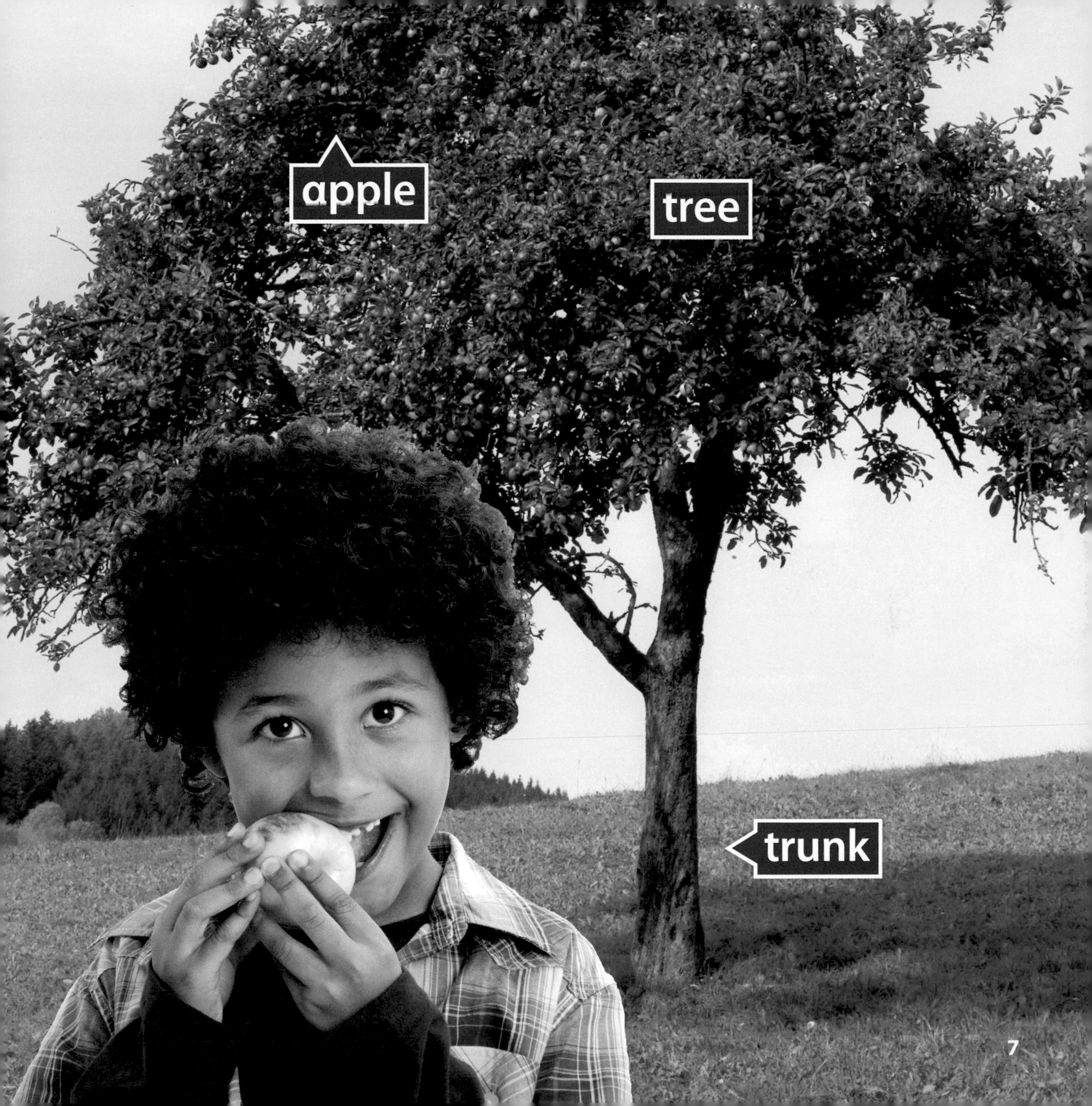
apple
tree
trunk

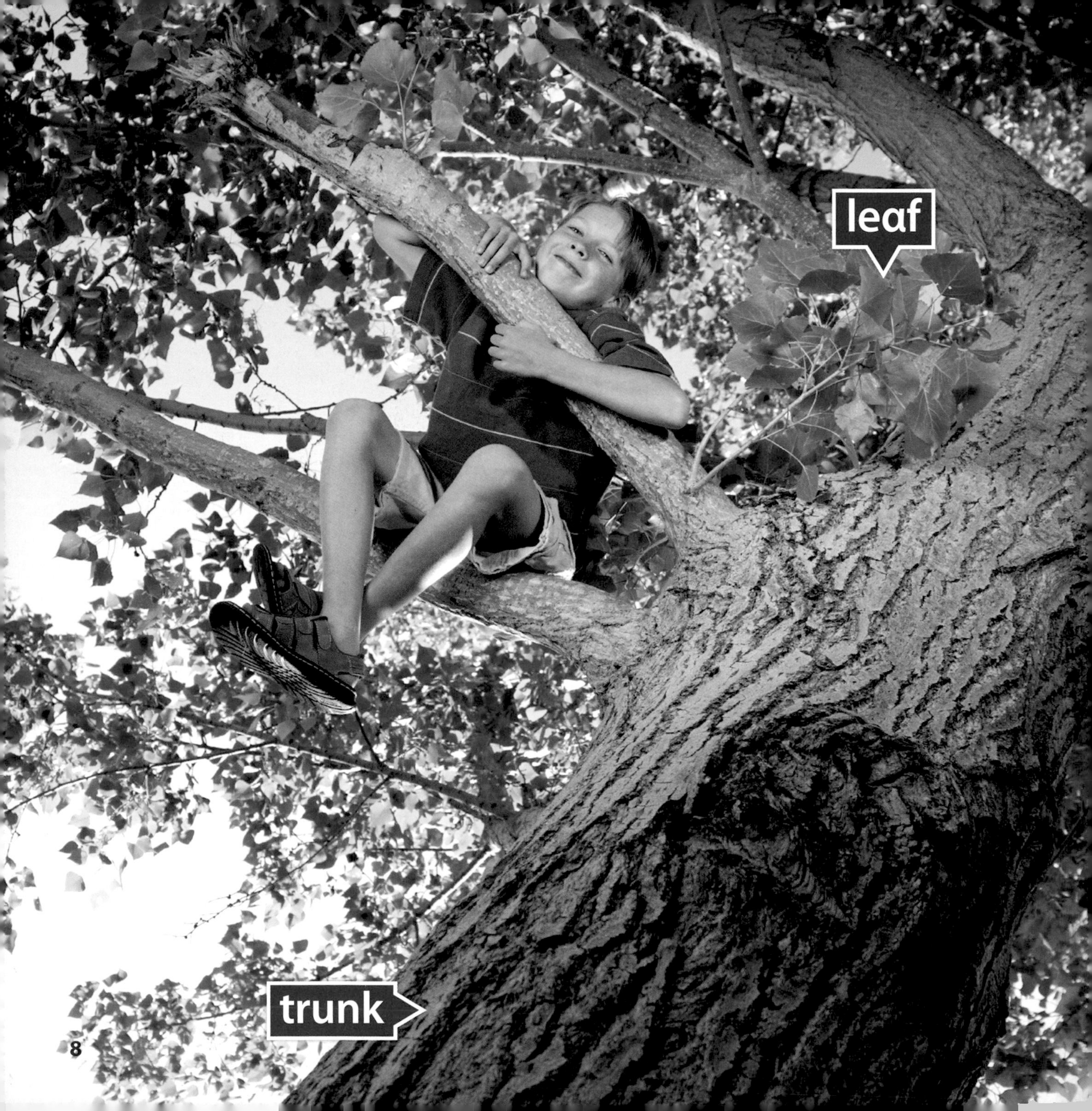
leaf
trunk